SHATTERED

Denise Byers

DanDeeLionPublishing

Copyright © Denise Byers 2018

Published by DanDeeLion Publishing
3 Way Street
Whitby, Ontario L1M 1B3
905-213-3919 / info@dandeelionpublishing.com

All rights reserved. No part of this publication may be reproduced, stored in a retrieval system, or transmitted in any form by any process – electronic, mechanical, photocopying, recording, or otherwise - without the prior written permission of the copyright owner and DanDeeLion Publishing. The scanning, uploading and distribution of this book via the Internet or via any other means without the permission of the copyright owner and publisher is illegal and punishable by law. Please purchase only authorized electronic editions, and do not participate in, or encourage, electronic piracy of copyrighted materials. Your support of the author's rights is appreciated.

Cover Design: Zach Timbers
Author Photo: Nikeshia Ducent

Library and Archives Canada
Cataloguing in Publication

Byers, Denise author
Shattered / Denise Byers

Issued in print and electronic formats
ISBN (paperback):   978-0-9880952-4-3
ISBN (epub):   989-0-9880952-5-0

This book is dedicated to my mother, Elizabeth "Liz" Byers, for her unwavering support, indescribable patience and steadfast love.

My Guardian Earth Angel

There are angels that walk among us.
Some carry us through the most difficult
Parts of our journey.

It's so hard to believe that someone can have
The strength that you so desperately need
Yet so disappointingly lack.

Thank you for keeping me safe in the folds of your
Beautiful wings and not letting me fall.
Most of all I thank you for reminding me that
Strong or weak, I am always loved.

I promise when I am the strong one
And you need to be carried,
I will bring out my wings and
Whisk you away to where and how
You need to be – safe and happy.

Mother, you are my angel and I am yours if you'll have me.

Love,
Denise

Contents

1. Dear Children
2. Inspiration
3. Don't Give Up
4. Little Princess D
5. Little Miss Dazey
6. Little Girl Lost
7. Fade Away to Grey
8. The Pity Party
9. Rollercoaster
10. Anxiety
11. Desperation
12. Hide and Seek
13. Mind Games
14. The Hacker
15. The Asylum
16. The Puzzle House
17. Lockdown
18. Caught in the Maze
19. Mama Said
20. Emptiness
21. At Least I Said Goodbye
22. I'm Shrinking
23. Slipping
24. Wallowing
25. Trapped
26. Collateral Damage
27. Irrational Fear
28. I Live But I'm Not Alive
29. Weeping on Heaven's Floor
30. Living in the Dark
31. Lonely
32. I Never Thought
33. Loss
34. Loneliness
35. My Secret
36. Broken Trust
37. They Call it The Blues
38. Courage to Cry
39. I Can't Stand the Pain
40. My Saviour
41. Frankly Speaking
42. You Left With No Goodbye
43. Put Your Hand in Mine
44. Blindsided
45. Fighting
46. A Fork in the Road
47. I've Got No Fear
48. I'm Perfectly Imperfect
49. Dear Princess
50. My Angel
51. The Attitude of Gratitude
52. Anguish and Clarity
53. Warrior Princess
54. Choose Life
55. International Help Lines

Dear Children:

In my darkest times of need
You've always been there
Giving me support
Showing how much you care.

I want to thank you
For this gift so priceless
I know it's been hard
I'm not always the nicest.

When I call out your name
You always show up
You never let me down
You're never harsh or abrupt.

Your compassion & patience
Has kept me afloat
I wish I could give you
More than this thank you note.

Please accept this small token
Of my immense gratitude
For everything you are
And everything you do.

If there's ever a day
I can do the same for you
Just call out my name
I'll be there for you too.

With eternal love
You help my heart sing
I'm ready to soar
You've given me wings.

Inspiration

I know a man
Who is standing in his truth
He has found his purpose
And mapping his own route.

He is walking in his own path
On his journey to his higher self
Along the way sharing knowledge
And inspiring us with good mental health.

He is generously lighting his path
For others to follow in his steps
To peace, joy and health
Wishing everyone the best.

As I watch him with awe
I find I admire this man.
Doing what I can't do,
I desire to take his hand.

Share your secrets with me.
Shower me in your glow.
Share some of your strength with me.
Teach me the way to go.

I am my worst enemy.
I can't get out of my own way.
To follow this man of inspiration
To a more successful way.

I struggle to know why.
I attempt to understand
Why I sabotage myself...
Why I'm not like this man.

Shine on my friend
As I stumble in your shadow.
Teach me to plant inspirational seeds
In a field of dreams that is so fallow.

Don't Give Up

I don't want you to put down this book
And feel like there is no chance for you to survive.
Mental illness is real; it just needs to be treated
So you can navigate it and feel alive, wanted and needed.

Little Princess D

Her golden crown slightly askew
Little Princess D grew and grew.
She worked too hard and she was never lazy.
She worked so hard her brain became hazy.
They all said Princess D had the blues.
That wasn't even half of the news.
Her life, though regal, was painful and sad.
It didn't matter how much she had;
She could never find happiness, not even a tad.
Some speculated, she'd simply gone mad.
Her emotions were tangled;
From a wall her feet dangled.
She succumbed to her demons and felt a bit crazy.
It was then Little Princess D became Little Miss Dazey.

Little Miss Dazey

Little Miss Dazey
She fell from the wall
And let me tell you,
It was one hell of fall.

Oh our Little Miss Dazey,
Oh, she sure did take a fall
And now she's shattered in pieces
Scattered behind her self-built wall.

All the King's horses
And all the King's men
Couldn't put Miss Dazey
Together again.

Yet, they all gathered around her
Said all of the right things:
"You'll be fine in good time dear;
You'll be dancing through rings!"

When she's healed she'll visit.
"She's doin' great", they'll agree;
But they'll all be blind to the "she"
That only she seems able to see.

Her mind is getting hazy.
Her paralysis called lazy.
It's a short trip to crazy.
Oh, who wants to drive Miss Dazey?

It's not far to the Puzzle House
Where all the pieces reside;
Where they're supposed to link together
So you no longer have to hide.

You better bring the glue though;
You know the one that's crazy,
Because these pieces aren't gonna click
Her mind, it does amaze me.

She balanced on the edge of that wall;
But before she stumbled, they couldn't tell
That Little Miss Dazey was struggling
Because she sure did hide it well.

Oh our Little Miss Dazey,
She sure did take a fall;
And now she's shattered in pieces
Scattered behind her self-built wall.

Little Girl Lost

Little girl lost
Oh so forlorn
Another lost soul
For us to mourn.

Little Miss Dazey,
Our little girl lost
What will become of her
And what will be the cost?

An unhappy nine year old
Masquerading, if you will
As a full grown woman
Who's totally fulfilled.

How long can the charade last
Before people find out
The woman that sits before them
Is a girl who desperately wants out?

And will the world collapse
If she shatters and breaks
Because of the adult burdens
That her soul cannot take?

So there's Miss Dazey
Dangling stiletto from the wall.
Material life had been good to her
Until they took it all.

They even took her dignity,
Her laughter and sense of fun.
Now her passion for living
Is something, from which she runs.

Will she shatter?
Will she break?
Has life finally given her
More than she can take?

Little Miss Dazey
Our little girl lost
What will become of her
And what will be the cost?

Fade Away to Grey

Why can't I ever get it right?
I think I'm just gonna hide away
Why isn't everything black and white?
I'll find comfort in the grey.
Goals I have, but don't follow through
I think I'm just gonna hide away
If I can't reach my goals soon
I'll find comfort in the grey.
Feelings aren't wrong; feelings aren't right
I think I'm just gonna hide away.
Feelings aren't cut; feelings aren't dried
I'll find comfort in the grey.
My mind is confused; paralyzed in fear
I think I'm just gonna hide away.
I can't find the old me; life's not how it should be
I'm fading away to grey.

The Pity Party

I don't think anyone understands
How hard it is to be perpetually sad.
No break from the darkness ever
No laughter or light to be had.

It's permanent grief.
It's the mourning of the loss of who you used to be
It's the wanting to turn back time
To the morning before darkness was all you could see.

The longing for who you were
Never subsides or goes away.
The knowing you'll never be her again
Makes it harder to face each day.

When I chose this life
I bit off more than I can chew.
Now I'm sitting here asking
What in the world am I gonna do?

There's a pity party being thrown for me
And you are all invited.
You'll meet my nearest and dearest friends
But don't be too excited.

Depression and Loneliness will be there
And of course they'll bring the twins, Doom & Gloom.
Those two follow me everywhere
To ensure nothing good will ever bloom.

"Oh My, it hasn't been that long", I'll say,
"But look how much they've grown!"
"Doom and Gloom have gotten so big!"
And they still won't leave me alone.

As I sit in the dark, paralyzed by fear
I consider my tomorrows.
I muster the courage to count my blessings
And toss out my cup of sorrows.

It's time to dust off Loneliness
And put Depression on the back shelf,
Scare Doom and Gloom away with light
And start taking care of myself.

When I chose this life
I bit off more than I can chew
Now I'm sitting here - content
But do you know what I've been through?

Rollercoaster

I hide in my room
Dripping in sweat from anxiety
Afraid to leave my bed
This terror of a special variety.

The bills are rolling in
A new one every day
The amounts astronomical
How will I ever pay?

Clouds between my knees
Two weeks ago I was riding high
Laughing uncontrollably
I was surfing the sky!

I couldn't stop talking
So animated when I landed
I was still flying high
Some say I was manic.

My credit cards declined
I had finally crashed.
No friends with whom to party
When I ran out of cash.

Now as I lie here and reflect
On my life and how I sank it
I pull the covers over my head
I can't breathe, all I can do is panic.

I hate taking the pills
They make me feel so numb.
I want to feel everything
Even if it sounds dumb.

But this rollercoaster ride
Well it's getting old.
The panic driven sweat on my skin
Is making me cold.

I'll have to face the music
Sooner than later.
Time to ask for help
So I can get better.

Anxiety

Up down
Up down
Round and round
Round and round
Flying high
Crash to the ground
Know you're worthless
When your fall makes no sound
Up again
Riding high
Feeling manic
Start to panic
Overnight rants
Wish I could forget
Mornings of remorse
And regrets
Bringing on anxiety sweats
Must face the backlash
Moods swinging so fast
I get whiplash
Now rushing to
Hit delete
Wondering who saw
Mistakes I don't want to repeat
It's out of my control
I give up
Wash, rinse, repeat.

Desperation

I'm trapped in my head
Figuratively strapped to my bed.

Drowning in my anxious perspiration
As I try to claw my way out of desperation.

Inexplicably scared of what's ahead
What might happen if I get out of bed.

I know my fears are unfounded
That's what's got me so damned confounded.

What happened to the go getter?
The once confident jet setter?

Where did I go? Why do I hide?
They say it's mental illness but I'm mystified.

They say I need to be fixed
Yet, I remain perplexed.

When did I slip into such desperation
To conquer inexplicable fears & depression?

I look in the mirror
And I just don't see her.

A frightened stranger glares back at me
Her eyes holding a desperate plea.

All I can say is "I'm sorry"
And back to my bed, I flee.

Hide and Seek

Would you like to play a game?
It's called hide and seek
But I forewarn you, I'll win
Because you don't know the real me.

So polished and poised
Just to get through each day
But it's fake interest & fake smiles
I'm phony in every way.

The rules are you have to find the "me" that you know
On the count of 100, it's your turn to go.
When you find "me", we'll giggle and laugh
Until I pull off my beautifully perfected mask.

Then you'll see darkness and the true despair
I'm sure you'll express concern and deep honest care.
You'll be confused and surely incited to help me by your fears
But it's too late for that my friend
I've already drowned in a puddle of my tears.

Mind Games

Mesmerized by the game of illusion
Stumbling through the fog of confusion
Living my own life feeling like it's an intrusion
Playing a game that I just keep on losin'
Suspecting I'm the victim of collusion
Maybe it's all just a delusion.

The Hacker

I've been robbed! I've been robbed!
My life has been snatched!
Over 50 years together
And my husband's mind has been hacked!

To look at him
He looks the same
Same smile, same laugh
He answers to his own name.

But when I really look
Deeply into his eyes
I can see he is wearing
A brilliant disguise.

He pretends to know who I am
But it's all a grand charade
He may fool others
But I am watching him fade.

Drifting slowly but surely
Into a massive abyss
Forgetting his loved ones
I pray ignorance is bliss.

He may be easily unaware
Of the tears we cry and hide
Or he may feel frustrated & embarrassed
Or as guilty as I.

He's now in a safe place
But it isn't our home
I wake startled every morning
Wondering why I'm awaking alone.

I give my head a shake
I say "this is our new life"
I feel lonely & abandoned
Alzheimer's now his wife.

I'm adjusting to my new normal
Stumbling in the dark. There's no light.
My life has been stolen
By a disease that is truly, a thief in the night.

The Asylum

A place where you're the sane one
Where the inmates run the asylum
We let them think they are in charge
It's so funny how easy it is
To lie to them.

The Puzzle House

They're taking me to a place I know
A place where they make you sane
I'm still missing a piece of life's puzzle
So they're taking me back again.

It's a box of minds of malfunction
Together in a house of dysfunction
Brains unbalanced by chemical corruption
We're leading lives of interruption.

My brain chemistry is so corrupted
That now I'm a girl interrupted.

I cannot mature: I cannot grow
I can barely get out of bed.
I'm surrounded by bars & guards
I don't know how this is helping my head.

They give me pails of pills
That I hide under my tongue
Because I watch my unhinged roomies
Wander the halls looking stunned.

Will I turn out like them?
My brain drugged & electrocuted?
Because if I will, hear me now
I'd rather be executed!

I don't want to hide from reality
Hide behind pills and pillowed walls
I want to face my demons
But I'm afraid of how far I'll fall.

In here, they're all crazier than me,
In the Puzzle House, I'm the Queen of the Castle
The real world is a different thing;
On the outside, I'm the crazy rascal.

Lockdown

I'm in lockdown
Self-imposed exile...
Just me, myself and Denial!

I'm in lockdown
In good company...
Denial, myself and ME!

I'm in lockdown
Oh YES!
Self-imposed house arrest!

No one can get to me
Everyone will leave me be!
They'll compare me to Amy and Britney
But I just wanna figure out ME!

Caught In The Maze

So many questions, to which I don't have the answers
I never thought this is where I would be
At this point in my life journey
I started out small with big dreams
And before I knew it, bubbles were bursting
And nothing is the way it seems.

I'm all cashed out; I've completely crashed out
I've totally trashed my life & strewn it all about
Now I thrash in my sleep trying to figure a way out.
Oh, there's gotta be an easier way!
There's gotta be a map to this amazing maze.

There's gotta be a way to see through this thick haze.
The haze of fear, the haze of doubt;
But the wardens of shame & guilt guard this drought.
It needs to rain. Oh, how I wish it would pour.
So I can stop struggling to find the door.

I need out of here to start my life over
Failure wasn't part of my vision.
I'll keep dreaming big because dreams are still free
That is my decision.

Mama Said

I never thought this is where I'd be
I never thought it could happen to me.
But here I am; lost and alone
Nowhere to go; don't have a home.

Mama told me once that God doesn't give you
More than you can handle
But Mama, what if this one
Can't be solved by lighting a candle?

Let God lead you child
My Mama said to me
He'll never lead you astray
My Mama guaranteed.

God and I aren't on speaking terms
Mama told me to pray anyway.
He'll come through for you Dear.
He won't let you go too far away.

I don't think he hears me Mama
I pray and pray night and day
She said, You might not like the answers, Dear
But sometimes that's just the way.

I've done some bad things
I'm a sinner's sinner
Maybe I can't be saved
I'm not a life lottery winner.

Mama said, He hears you Dear
Don't think that way.
No matter how tough life is
God won't lead you astray.

But I have gone astray
And no matter how much I pray
My mistakes won't go away
Will God forgive me anyway?

Mama said God forgives us all
No matter how far and hard we fall.
Mama said I've gotta believe
Or I will never get my reprieve.

So my attitude now is
Believe so I achieve
Dreams I've held deep down
And want to retrieve.

Emptiness

I'm all out of wisdom to share
Even though I still care
It's just that now I'm the one who is revealing my despair.
I know with all my heart that I can't love myself here but I will over there.
This is the end of this show.
It's time to take a new one on the road.
I took my time here so you'd know
That I've always loved you so.
Please know I cried as I tried
To keep myself alive.
Instead of choosing to die
I stayed on our ride.
So I could be here for you
I did all I could do
You might not believe that, but it is true.
Sadly there's no cure for a life that turned the darkest shade of blue.
Too many to count
Of who I let down.
I've cried the tears of a clown
Trying to fool those around;
But, you're too smart to not see
I failed to make it the good life every life should be.
I now need you to understand that I need to be free.
It's not you making me leave, that is on me.
My soul needs to soar.
Life's shaken me to the core.
I need to escape the uproar
By simply walking through that door.
Maybe one day you'll forgive
Understand why I couldn't live
A life not festive
Regardless of all that I did.
Please stay tuned,
It's a life to be continued
To keep loving you
Deep down you know I truly do.
I just cannot stay
Time's up, it's judgment day.
The angels will come and take me away.

All I can say
Is that I hope that one day
You won't think of me with hate
Because I was a fake
A soul too weak to take
The burdens life put on me
Stealing the happy version everyone could see.
I hope I gave you at least one good memory
For you to find solace in place of me.
It's time to jump off my wall
Allow myself one final fall
Show's over, this is my final curtain call.
As the light fades, I still see you all.
With my unmasked frown
I know I let you down.
I'm on my knees on the ground
As I make this final vow
To guide you and love you as I do now.

Please forgive me.

At Least I Said Goodbye

For those of you who said I didn't fight
Learn that your words can really bite

For those who called me a drama queen
Know you were just really mean

Every time I was met with a blank stare
Know how much I was really scared

Know every time you rolled your eyes
It was met with silent cries

For those who tried to hide your fed up sighs
Know you just made me truly want to die

You've never seen what I have seen
You've certainly never been where I have been

You've never endured debilitating pain
Every time it simply rained

You've never had the kind of stress
That makes a life one hot mess

This is no way to live
So when I die, I pray that you can forgive

Know I really didn't want to go
Because I love you all so

I know some of you don't believe
That I really didn't want to leave

And I'm just putting on my princess crown
To see what pity I can arouse

Know for every one of those thoughts
I knew you didn't think of me as a whole lot

For those of you I truly love
Know that I will guide you from above

Know that I will miss your touch
Because I love you so goddamned much

For those of you who truly love me
All I can say is that I am sorry

But existing in the world this way
Doesn't make me want to stay

I feel I'm being punished in the most inhumane way
For what, I sincerely can't say

I'm sorry if I've let you down
But with this anguish, I can't stick around

I hope one day you'll believe
That I really didn't want to leave

I know it's hard to wrap your head around
But I am lost and need to be found

That isn't going to happen here on earth
Apparently zero is what my life is worth

I need to be able to break free
And hope you'll remember me fondly

Now it's time to say goodbye
For those of you who care, please don't cry

Please do not weep for me
For I am finally turmoil free.

I'm Shrinking

I get my head shrunk at least four times a year.
Slowly but surely, I'm beginning to disappear.

I take the happy pills I am given
But my brain chemistry levels haven't risen.

Every night I'm afraid I'll awaken
Soaked in anxiety sweat and shakin'.

The head shrinker looks at me with care
Then pats my head and says "there, there."

The shrink placates and medicates
Then suggests I go home and meditate.

Invisible is my pain and anguish
So I'm pumped with pills and left to languish.

The mental healthcare system
Doesn't speak or understand my language
My health care is nothing but a mere bandage.

What's in store for me long term?
I sit in a waiting room anxious to learn.

Still no answers come
I am quickly becoming numb.

Mental illness is like any other disease
Would the mental healthcare system help me please.

Slipping

I feel like I'm slipping under water
I'm gonna touch the bottom of the sea
I feel like I'm slipping under water
I'm outta breath, no one to save me

I feel like I'm slipping under water
I'm reaching up hoping for a hand
Someone to pull me out of the water
Pull me out and back onto land

I feel like I'm slipping under water
Don't have any air left in me
Don't think many care that I won't be there
Once I'm gone, their lives will be happy

They pretend to care
But no one is there
Having said that, no one said
My life would be fair

So maybe I should slip under water
Stop reaching out and pleading for help
No one is coming; they don't really care
They don't want to understand poor mental health.

I feel like I'm slipping under water
I no longer want to be back on land
So save me your platitudes that make you feel better
Pockets were designed for unwilling hands.

Wallowing

I appreciate your kind advice
But I'm afraid I'd rather wallow
Everything you say makes sense
It's just too hard to swallow.
I used to have dreams
They could still come true
Yet something stops me
From following through.
I've lost my drive
Even my reasons to live
It's hard to understand
I just hope you can forgive.
I don't know what it is
This thing that holds me back
I have the time and ability
Then I self attack.
Self sabotage is my game
I stop myself
The closer I get
To making myself a name.
I have the talent and time
I have the resources and skill
I also have the ability
To ensure my happiness I kill.
Is it fear of failure?
Is it fear of success?
All I know
Is that I'm not doing my best.
I'm sorry I disappoint you
I seem to have a compulsive obsession
To behave and think in a way
That ensures my depression.
I know you don't understand
Hell, neither do I.
I awake every morning
Glued to my bed asking myself why.

Trapped

I'm trapped in the sick machinations
Of my own troubled mind
The trap door exit
Not so easy to find.

They wanna fill me with meds
But I'd rather be dead
Than depend on pills
To get me outta my head.

Some sufferers stick to the booze
And have drunken rants
Unbalanced inside; stick to what
They can do, not what they can't.

I'll live in my house of cards
Waiting for the wolf at my door
To blow my house down
I don't expect anything more.

I need to block out the voices
In my head so I can think
But I need a little help
And the solution is not a drink.

That trap door is somewhere
I'll make my escape
Cannibalistic thoughts are eating my mind
Soon, my soul they will take.

I'm running out of time
Gotta balance my mind
Need to drown out the voices
My escape I shall find.

Collateral Damage

A total stranger stared blankly at her
When they sent her husband back
Her smile quickly turned to despair
As they stood awkwardly by the train tracks.

They called it "shell shock"
And maybe that was so
They returned a shell of a man
Horror ripped him of his soul.

We are rightfully grateful for
Those who have died
But how many recognize the sacrifices
Of those who survived?

The only constant that I see with schizophrenia
Is that it can take different forms
As it thunders through your life with
Lightning and torrential rain storms.

This disease robbed so many
People in his life
He had mental health issues
He blamed on his wife.

A tumultuous marriage
Producing wonderful kids
They appeared to have it all
And in a way, they did.

It was a home that could be tense
All because of this "invisible" disease
With symptoms
That even doctors wouldn't believe.

It was also a loving home
It wasn't filled with blame
At its core, it was fun and happy
All proudly living without shame.

Not every schizophrenic gets treatment
They don't always believe
That they need help
To manage this legitimate disease

This man has long passed but
He'd be happy today you can call for help
And someone at the other end of that phone
Would work with you toward good mental health.

Irrational Fear

I am strong
But I'm not invincible.
I'm here
I am not invisible.

Look at me!
Hear my words.
I'm a whole person,
Not two thirds.

My heart is not made of steel,
But it's protected by a brick wall
Yet you still find a way to hurt me;
I've gotta find & patch that hole.

There's a hole in my wall
And you're poking me through it.
I don't understand
Why you do it?

Does it please you
When I cry?
Then I have to ask
Why? Just why?

Is it because you can feel me
Shake in fear of things that aren't real,
My anxiety pulsating throughout my being
You knowing I'm mentally ill?

You're gone, where did you go?
I've turned away from my mirror
You didn't answer my questions
So my mind isn't any clearer.

Could you be a voice inside the looking glass
And never were really here?
Could it be my true reality
And my troubled mind that I fear?

I Live But I Am Not Alive

I heard you weren't vengeful
I heard you didn't judge
I heard you were forgiving
I heard you didn't hold a grudge.

The evidence doesn't bear out that myth
I'm in turmoil every minute of every day
And there you are with power you won't use
To make it all go away.

I thought life was supposed to be LIVED
And not just survived;
But, here I am. I merely exist
I live but I am not alive.

Do you enjoy watching me suffer?
Do you like seeing me in pain?
Does it make you laugh when I cry,
Over and over again?

So many sheep worship you
Up there on your throne.
Down here, I hold my head in anguish
In pain, I moan and groan.

You obviously have something against me
But, can't we work it out?
I pray for your help every night
Do you hear me as I shout?

You claim to be God, but I think you're a fraud
What crime did I commit to deserve this sentence?
Do I get a reprieve or am I just naïve
To believe your existence is not just a pretense?

I'm angry, I'm sad; I'm frustrated, I'm mad.
I don't understand what I'm supposed to gain
By living each and every day
In life-draining, excruciating pain.

Help me please, I'm begging you.
Please put me out of my misery.
Help me start over pain free.
Help me re-write my history.

I need the help of the Wizard,
For surely, I'm in Oz
Where this pain-filled life is all a dream
And will soon be back to what it was.

I live but truthfully, I just exist
It's getting harder to survive.
I'm begging you for a chance
For my life to be revived.

So I click my heels and say the lines
Take away this debilitating life I am living
I'm also giving you a chance to prove
You're real & you're forgiving.

Weeping on Heaven's Floor

I'm losing hope
I'm losing faith
Does God even see me?
Does He recognize my face?

God has forgotten my address
He doesn't know where I live
And I've done so many bad things
That I need Him to forgive

But He doesn't know where to find me
Because I've locked my heart's door
Now I beg to lay before Him,
Weeping on Heaven's floor.

He's not taking my calls
He's not answering His door
So here I am weeping,
Weeping on Heaven's floor.

Living in the Dark

Someone flip the switch
For where there is light
Darkness can't exist.

Lonely

I'm surrounded by people;
Rarely alone
Yet I'm lonely most of the time
I just don't feel at home.

I Never Thought

I'm surrounded by people, rarely alone
I'm living in somebody else's home.
I never thought this was how it would be
I never thought this could happen to me.

I made some bad choices along the way
But I didn't think they'd affect me today.
If I could turn back the hands of time.
I'd make better decisions; my life would be mine.

I'm grateful for the help I've received,
But my life's out of control more than I could have ever believed.
I've given up on finding my one and only
I'm surrounded by people and yet I am lonely.

I want to make choices that are my own.
I want people to respect that I am grown.
I make better choices than I have in the past.
I need people to trust me not to finish last.

I feel so much shame, I feel so much guilt.
A wall of bricks around my heart I have built.
I need a special someone to just knock one out
And teach me to trust my gut without any doubt.

I need a compassionate, caring companion
So I don't feel alone in this giant canyon.
I have so much love that I need to give.
I have so much life left to live.

I never thought this was how it would be.
I never thought this could happen to me.
I never thought I wouldn't be free.
I never thought I could be this lonely.

Loss

It's depression
That's making me sadder
Grief, sorrow & heartache
Making me madder

Cancer took my friends
And the pain never ends
It's a feeling that
Just won't go away

Because there's nobody left in this world
To hold me tight
And there's nobody left in this world to
Make it all right

God took my loves
To His heaven above
And He told me that
I had to stay

Now I'm lonely as hell
And I'm not feeling well
Though I know I'll see my friends
Again some day

Sadly, this doesn't give me much solace
My mental stability seems to be the cost
Of such brutal reminders of life's fragility
With each and every loss.

Loneliness

Nothing matters anymore,
The present has no hope.
The past is best forgotten,
The future has no meaning.

Why should I care?
My life is like an empty room;
No amusement, no happiness,
Excitement is unheard of.

What is it all worth?
Who needs this deprivation?
I'm not getting anything for this,
To HELL with living!

Nothing matters anymore.
Why should I care?
What is it all worth?
I give up.

My Secret

Got a secret
It's hard to keep it
Oh I hate my lonely life
My best friend's a loaded gun
I keep by my side
I'm afraid I'm gonna lose it
Cuz then I'm gonna choose it
One pull of the trigger
A big bang and bye bye.

Broken Trust

Oh all my dear ones
You all used to be able
To trust me more than anyone
Until that trust, I disabled.

I broke that trust twice this year
By trying to kill myself.
You gave me a second chance
And time to get back my health.

I tried to walk the line for you
But the second suicide attempt
Brought on confusion & conflict
Distrust and contempt.

I thought about being gone forever
What if I never came back?
I'm trying to walk the line again
But what if my enthusiasm doesn't come back?

The paralyzing fears
And uncontrollable tears
Are bringing on the years
Escape's ugly head rears.

As cannibalistic thoughts
Are devouring my mind
I'm fighting with all I have
To keep my will to survive.

There is no sweet escape
From your reality
You learn to cope, you learn to hide
It's such a duality.

They Call it The Blues

There's something I need to tell you
Some say it's the blues every day
I'm being ripped apart inside
By mental illness in every way.

I'm clinically depressed
But some say it's just the blues
I've been disillusioned, dismissed and discounted
I'm hurt and I feel confused.

I won't take anymore abuse
I'm fed up with struggle and strife
I don't want another excuse
I'm done with this life.

Courage to Cry

I had so many chances to let you in
To share the secrets that I hide
But would you still have loved me
If you knew how many demons I buried inside?

I didn't know and couldn't take the chance
So I kept my secrets & feelings to myself
It didn't feel like I was deceiving you
Because I was lying to me & everyone else.

I couldn't show you that fragile side
I had my dignity; I had my pride
I only wish I'd also had
The courage so you could see me cry.

You should know I never meant to hurt you
It's just the way my brain is wired
If I'd just been strong enough to lean on you
I wouldn't be so tired.

We'd still be together today
If I hadn't been living a lie
I wish I had accepted my mental illness
I wish I'd had the courage to cry.

I mask my pain with seething anger
And the hurt has less sting to it
I take my anger out on others
And don't even realize I do it.

I lash out at others because I'm never sad
Apparently, I have two emotions: happy & mad
That's how I roll; that's my M.O.
Only I'm the only one who doesn't seem to know.

Now I strike back at suicidal thoughts
Head pounding; stomach in knots.
I'd rather die and don't know why
I simply can't muster the courage to cry.

I Can't Stand The Pain

I can't stand the pain
God's asked me to endure.
I can't stand the pain
For which there is no cure.

The war wages on inside my body
It wages on inside my mind.
Searching for a solution
No one can seem to find.

They say it will be over soon
But that gives me little relief.
I hope I'll be better soon
All I've got left is belief.

Maybe when we get together again
I'll be feeling so very well.
I'll escort you into Heaven
There will be no more Hell.

I can't bear this mental illness
I pray you understand
Years from now when you join me
I'll be there to take your hand.

My Saviour

The monsters were winning
The demons inside me were fierce
I was fighting so hard not to relinquish myself
Trying hard to overcome my fears.
I accidentally tipped off my sister
Or I'd have been gone a decade ago
I didn't think she'd be able to tell
I didn't think she would know
I swallowed a bunch of pills
And I was drifting off to sleep
But from five hours away she called 911
Sensing my depression had run too deep
I was angry at the time
Oh I was mad as hell
How dare she interrupt my plan
How dare she ring the warning bell.
They got here just in time
I was surely slipping away
I look back at my actions now
And that life changing day.
I once again knew my sister loved me
You see, we had drifted apart
But now I knew she wanted me to live
I didn't know I still held a place in her heart.
Thank you, Amanda for saving my life
It got me the medical help I needed
It took some time but the pain and
Mental anguish had receded.
I still need your support
I still need your love
Because some days I still feel
I'd rather die. I've had enough.

Frankly Speaking

Crack!
A thunderous noise in the night.
She sat up in the bed bolt right

Look!
He wasn't in the bed beside her
An ominous vibe grew inside this fighter

Alarm!
The ringing pierced her tired ears
His absence brought forth more fears

Shock!
Bullets sprinkled on the table
An invisible force pulled her to the stable

Punch!
She nearly toppled to the ground
Startled by the gruesome scene she found

Scream!
Her tears drowning out the sound
No one could hear her for miles around

Sirens!
Blaring sounds and dizzying lights
So unnecessary, he was gone that night.

Doubt!
Replaying the moments in her head
Should she have called 911 from her bed?

Breathe!
She knew deep down when she heard that crack
That he was never coming back.

Resignation!
He took his own life with a trigger's click
She couldn't have saved him. He was mentally sick.

Grief!
She mourned him deeply in that harsh daylight
But she knew he had to do what he thought was right.

Guilt!
She wishes he had asked for help
But we are all responsible for our own mental health

Fight!
She was scrutinized and criticized
She knew the truth. THEY should have apologized.

Onward and Upward!
Eventually the scene pushed to the back of her mind
She sought a life of a different kind.

Silence!
Her tears had finally dried
She had mourned; she had cried

Bang!
With a big bang a new existence took shape
She finally moved on, letting the haters hate.

Boom!
Leaving the ghosts of the past in the darkness of night
She made it through to the light; BOOM, drop the mic!

You Left With No Goodbye

I just don't understand
Why you had to leave
You could've stuck around
You could've gotten a reprieve.

You decided to go
You know you had a choice
Why'd you have to do it?
Where was your voice?

I take solace in the memories
We made lovingly together.
I guess we were naive
To think that we'd last forever.

Because everybody's day comes
When they are asked to go.
But you left with no goodbye,
And oh that hurt me so.

You made the decision
To end your anguish on your own...
Seeking a sweet escape
Begging to go Home.

If there's nothing else you hear,
Know that I'm sad but I understand
Depression and anxiety got the best of you
And you took your life and death into your own hands.

I wish you hadn't done it
I wish you'd reached out to me
I would have helped you to see
The wonderful person you are and have always been.

Put Your Hand In Mine

When it gets so incredibly dark
Your false saviour will appear
Shining false light that is not holy
Deceiving you, promising to end your fear.

You are weak from mental illness
Prey to this demon's trickery
These are the things you will hear
Don't believe them; it's not your victory.

And the demon will sing:

Put your hand in mine
It will be just fine
Let me show you the way
To a brighter day.

Let me keep you close
So you won't be alone
Put your hand in mind
And I will lead you Home.

They sent me from above
So that you could know true love
Put your hand in mine
We'll follow the peace dove.

Say goodbye to dark clouds
Say goodbye to the rain
Put your hand in mine
I will guide you through the pain.

They will understand
You've been called up by the Man
Put your hand in mine
I'll lead you to the Promise Land.

You've overcome all your challenges
Your work on Earth is done
I'm here to bring you Home
To good health, peace and fun.

Lies, lies, lies!
This "saviour" is a fake
You will know your true salvation
When you no longer feel your heart break.

Do not take his hand
Do not follow his lead
He's a quick tongued serpent
Sent only to deceive.

He will encourage you to take your life
With your very own hand
God would never ask this of you
To reach the true promise land.

When you see the false light of hope
Resist the urge to follow this prankster
Know it is time to reach out for help
Because suicide is never the answer.

Blindsided

It's so hard to put the past
Behind you and keep it there
Brightly lit reminders seem
To blindside you just when you
Are getting there.

Fighting

I've been torn and tattered
Broken and batatered
Still I keep soldiering on.
Night after night
I fight the good fight
Resisting the demons' charms.
I dance with the dead
Suicidal thoughts in my head
Teetering on my wall.
I tell myself lies
I stifle my cries
I consider letting myself fall.
But something inside me
Something I can't see
Keeps me from ending it all.

A Fork in the Road

Once again, I've come to a fork in the road
I haven't made a right turn so far
So, do I take a quick left this time
Or will it just lead to one more scar?

I've made so many wrong turns
I've sped through this life
I got my tickets and paid my fines
I can't afford to do it wrong twice.

My confidence's stock is dropping
Every choice has its price
Do I fall into line and follow the pack
Or do I just throw the dice?

So how do I know what is the right path
The one that will lead me to salvation
How do I know where it will lead?
I need to build a solid foundation.

I'm looking back for a path forward
When I really need a change in direction
I'm so scared I'll go down the wrong path
At least with the past I have a connection.

I'm afraid of the road ahead
But I have to tear off the rearview mirror
I have to only look ahead
To find my healthy path with my vision clearer.

I've Got No Fear

I've been scrutinized
Been criticized
Gotten evil eyes
Been told lots of lies.

I don't mind.
Doesn't bother me.
Been through worse.
Confidence the key.

I've hit rock bottom,
But I'm a survivor and persevere
I can't be brought down
Because I've got no fear.

I'm into the positive,
No negativity.
Positivity the answer,
Confidence the key.

If you don't like me
That's ok too.
See, I was never
Counting on you.

When you've survived
All that I have,
All the naysayers
Just make you laugh.

Their giant egos...
Their petty feuds...
Are nothing compared
To what I've lived through.

Chronic pain, unrelenting sadness
Anxiety attacks that restrain you to your bed
Suicidal thoughts
Floating around inside your head.

I'm rising from rock bottom
I'm a survivor. I persevere
I can't be brought down
Because I've got no fear.

I'm Perfectly Imperfect

I made a mistake and drunk dialed
Then you answered the phone.
I begged you back & you told me gently
"Babe, you can't come back home".

Well we can't say we didn't try
And try and try again,
But practice only makes better
Not perfect, like we thought back then.

I'm flawlessly flawed
I'm perfectly imperfect.
I'm a child of God
I'm a girl interrupted.

I wish you knew me now
But you won't see perfection.
You'll still see my flaws
So adjust your expectations.

I now have clarity of mind & soul
And a protected open heart,
A fearlessness to take chances
The courage to make a new start.

I've gone through some changes
And think you'd be impressed.
I'm better than the "me", you knew
Although I'm still not the best.

I still mess up and make mistakes
But have much better judgment.
I make healthier decisions
I've made some serious lifestyle adjustments.

I'll always need treatment
For my mental illness
But I hope you'll try to trust me again,
All it takes is your willingness.

Dear Princess:

Please sit down
I've got a story to tell
But be forewarned
It doesn't end well...

Once upon a time
In a land far away
Lived a Princess who just
Couldn't find her way.

She'd take one step forward
Then two steps back
Though she tried & she tried
And her brain she did wrack.

Her feet felt like
They were stuck in cement
She cried and she cried
To others, she'd lament.

Eventually the Queen
Got fed up with her antics
She locked her in a dungeon
Princess soon became frantic.

Escape was always on her mind
But how would she get past her keeper?
She soon lost her will & accepted her fate
Depression came & Princess sunk deeper.

She analyzed herself almost to death
And filled her heart with hate
She drove herself crazy
The loneliness wouldn't abate.

Now Heaven won't have her
And Hell's afraid she'll take over
She's so fueled by anger that
Satan's scared of her!

So there she sits
One lifetime after another
She never found a way to escape
There was no knight in shining armour.

The moral of this story
Is this my friends
Don't let hate fill your heart
And always make amends.

Be sensitive to others
And kind to yourself
And when you need it
ASK FOR HELP!

My Angel

I've spent my whole life wishing and praying
For a man who is true
Then one day an Angel appeared
And that Angel, he was you.

At first I didn't think you were
The answer to my hopes and dreams
Until you wrapped me in your wings
And opened my heart at the seams

You brought me out of the dark
And opened my heart to the light
That's when I knew you were the answer
To those prayers I say each night.

I don't care what people say
You became my Angel that day.
I will be with you 'til the end of time;
'Til the end of reason, the end of rhyme.

Your feathers touched my soul
Like nothing else could
Your wings caught my breath
Like nothing else should.

You brought me out of the dark
And opened my heart to the light
That's when I knew you were the answer
To those prayers I say each night.

You're my sweet Angel to be adored
You're my sweet Angel, my reward
For all I have survived and all I have endured
You're my sweet saviour, Oh, My Lord

Thank you, God, for my Angel
He pulled me up to the surface
Thank you, God, for my sweet Angel
Through him, I found my purpose.

The Attitude of Gratitude (for Amanda)

These words are a special gift for you
Sent from deep down in my heart
I would never want harsh words
To tear our bond apart.

I never properly thanked you
For everything you have done
Since mental illness changed me
I have not been the same woman.

So I thank you now for being there
When I couldn't be.
For taking care of things
So thoughtful and lovingly.

I'm trying to help myself again
It starts with making amends
For things I did; things I said
To ensure we were no longer friends.

I'm treating my mental illness
I'm changing my whole attitude
I just want to express to you
Every ounce of my gratitude.

Anguish & Clarity

I heard there's a place
Beyond the clouds
Where everyone smiles
And no one frowns.

I want to go there
I want to be free
Of the shackles of pain
Life has thrust upon me.

You won't see me again
But I don't think you'll mind
I won't be your burden
Of any kind.

I hear there is magic
So I can see you
You won't see me
But you won't want to.

You'll be done with my whining
And all of my complaints.
You'll be happier without me
And I'll live among Saints!

I hear my soul
Will get a new lease
And over there, there's no turmoil
Just peace

It's just behind the curtain
Some call it a veil
Others call it Heaven
There, souls do not fail.

I think you'll be better off
Once I am gone
You'll be free of
My same old sad song.

You'll go there one day
When you are old
I can meet you at the Rainbow Bridge
So I've been told.

But do I really want to leave now?
What will I miss if I'm not with you here?
Milestones of loved ones
Is what I fear.

I'll be able to see your successes and special moments
But not able to share
And despite my struggles
You know I still care.

I'd still exist
But in spirit form
Anguish asks, "Do I want to leave now?"
Clarity answers "No, wait out the storm".

Warrior Princess

I am a warrior Princess
Hiding deep within
Now I'm paralysed with fear
Much to my chagrin
I'm trying to dig deep
To find my inner crown
But my world is so dark
No light to be found

Oh the air is so heavy
Today I'm finding it hard to breathe
The fog so thick I can't find my glow
I've gotta rev my engine
Gotta find my get up and go

Can't find my way out of here
They've cancelled my flight
Gotta find my way back
Gotta breathe again tonight

Barely breathing to exist
The air sits firmly on my chest
I'm too weak to inhale deeper
But I don't want to meet the Grim Reaper

This warrior Princess
Has finally found her crown and sword
The enemy within me
Can no longer be ignored

I take a deep breath
And dive deep into my soul
To breathe in the air
The air's that's so cold

This warrior Princess
Is starting to see some light
The lantern of hope
Is finally within my sight

Can't let the heavy air
Weigh me down one more night
I'm a warrior Princess
Who has reclaimed her fight

This warrior Princess has been buried alive
One short breath at a time
I've chosen to have a full life
Not content to merely survive

The warrior within me takes a breath so deep
That I'm heady
But with my found crown, shield and sword
I'm gonna hold myself steady

Using my sword to slice through the air
The same air I let weigh me down
I realized I forgot who I truly am
A warrior Princess who just couldn't find her crown

I found the air's not too heavy
In fact it is light
I had an irrational fear
I just needed to fight

It's all about perspective
You choose to see dark or light
Don't let the weight bury you.
Just breathe. You'll be alright

So when the air becomes too heavy
Do not despair
Look deep down inside yourself
Your warrior is there.

When you feel like you're at the end of your rope

Please know you're **NOT**; there is **ALWAYS HOPE**!

Life may leave you **HAZED**.

Life may leave you **CRAZED**.

But, given a chance,

Life will ALWAYS leave you AMAZED.

I **SEE** YOU. I **HEAR** YOU. I **FEEL** YOU. YOU ARE **NOT** ALONE.

CHOOSE LIFE!

About the Author

Denise Byers is an award-winning author, a poet and publisher.

An accomplished business woman, Denise has over 25 years of professional writing, public relations and government relations experience.

Denise is a graduate of York University with her Bachelor of Arts Degree in Sociology.

When she's not writing, Denise loves to read, dance, listen to music and spend time with her three adult children.

Denise lives in the Greater Toronto Area in Ontario, Canada.

International Help & Crisis Hotlines

Canada

- **Canada's National Suicide Prevention Hotline**
  1-833-456-4566

- **Canada's Kids' Help Line**
  1-800-668-6868

United States

- **United States National Suicide Prevention Hotline**
  1-800-273-8255

- **NAMI (National Association for Mental Illness)**
  1-800-950-6264

England

- **England National Suicide Prevention Hotline**
  08457-90-90-90

Scotland

- **Scotland National Suicide Prevention Hotline**
  0800-93-85-87

Ireland

- **Ireland National Suicide Prevention Hotline**
  08457-90-90-90

Switzerland

- **Switzerland National Suicide Prevention Hotline**
  +41(0)27-321-21-21

Denise Byers, BA (Author/Poet)
- shattered@dandeelionpublishing.com

DanDeeLion Publishing
Contact Information

Website:
www.dandeelionpublishing.com

Cover and Bookdesign:
design@zwadet.com

Facebook:
www.facebook.com/dandeelionpublishing

Email:
info@dandeelionpublishing.com

Twitter:
@Dandeelion1

Instagram:
@Dandeelion1

www.ingramcontent.com/pod-product-compliance
Lightning Source LLC
Chambersburg PA
CBHW052027290426
44112CB00014B/2409